Adrift in the Pacific

About Wise & Wide

- A systematic 6-level English reading program based on Lexile® measures
- Diverse and interesting topics chosen from the elementary curriculums of Korea and English speaking western countries
- Well-written books in various forms including fiction stories, descriptive texts, and classics retold
- The informative but original fiction stories grab your interest, leading to the easy and clear understanding of the educational content.
- Improve thinking skills with solid after-reading activities at all levels of the series.

Wise & Wide is a 6-level English reading program that consists of 60 books and each level is systematically divided by Lexile® measures. The Lexile® Framework for Reading is the most popular reading measuring system in American formal education curriculums and many English programs. Over 20 out of 50 states in the U.S. mark Lexile® measures directly on students' final report cards and over 300 well-known publishers adopt and use Lexile® measures.

Experience many kinds of readings written by professional writers from the U.S. and England. They used interesting topics that were carefully chosen after analyzing elementary curriculums from around the world including Korea, the U.S., England, and Australia among many others. Comprehensive after-reading activities including graphic organizers, speaking tasks, and After-reading Tests are ready for you.

Levels in the series and their corresponding Lexile® measures

Level	Lexile® measures	U.S. Grade
Level 1	Below 200L	Pre K - K
Level 2	190L - 400L	Lower Grade 1
Level 3	350L - 530L	Upper Grade 1
Level 4	420L - 650L	Grade 2
Level 5	520L - 940L	Grade 3 - 4
Level 6	830L - 1070L	Grade 5 - 6

* Smart Readers: Wise & Wide level 1 is applicable to the preschool level in the U.S.
* The source of the relationship between Lexile® measures and U.S. school grades: CCSS(Common Core State Standards) FOR ENGLISH LANGUAGE ARTS, APPENDIX A (2012, which is used by 45 states in the U.S.)

Topic List

	Level 1	Level 2	Level 3	Level 4	Level 5	Level 6
Book 1	Science>Biology: The hibernation of animals Story	Science>Biology: Living and nonliving things Story	Science>Biology> Animals & the Environment: Sea otters Story	Environment> Living with nature: The diver & the persimmon tree Story	Science>Biology> Animal: Amazing animals of the Amazon Story	Science>Biology: Germs, transmitted diseases Story
Book 2	Literature> World classics: Aesop's fables Story	Literature> Traditional fairy tale: Old tales about stones Story	Social Studies> Economy: To run a business to make and save money Story	Science>Biology> Plants: Photosynthesis Story	Science>Earth science: Earth's layers,earthquakes, volcanoes, and earth's atmosphere Report	Mathematics> Sequence: The golden ratio & the Fibonacci sequence Story
Book 3	Science>Physics: How shadows are formed Story	Literature> World classics: Peter Pan Story	Science>Scientific technology: Nanobots Story	Literature>Myths: World's creation stories Story	Literature> Legend: The story of King Arthur Story	Literature>Myths: Constellation myths Story
Book 4	Literature> Traditional literature: The Talmud Story	Science>Biology> Animal: Polar bears Story	Science>Biology> Animal: Mountain gorillas Story	Social Studies> Cultural anthropology: Amazing ancient cultures of the world Story	Science> Earth science: Clouds and weather Story	Literature> Human & animals: The friendship between a girl and a horse Story
Book 5	Social Studies> Ethics: Rules in daily life Story	Science>Biology: The five senses Report	Social Studies> Cultural anthropology: Astonishing festivals Report	Art>Music: Stories from two operas Story	Social Studies> World culture & history: The Renaissance Story	Sports> Board sports: Surfing & snowboarding Story
Book 6	Social Studies> World geography & travel: Tourist attractions around the world Story	Science>Biology> Animal: Dinosaurs Story	Science> Astronomy: The solar system Story	Social Studies> People: Three great people who overcame hardships Story	Science>Scientific technology: The wonderful world of robots Report	Art>Music: Composers of the Romantic Era Report
Book 7	Science> Space science: The life of astronauts Report	Social Studies> Cultural anthropology: Mythological monsters from around the world Report	Mathematics> Elementary mathematics: Numbers, measurement, shapes and data Report	Science & Social Studies> Technology & culture: Inventions from around the world Report	Art>Works of art: Famous paintings Report	Social Studies> Human & animals: Animals in action for human Report
Book 8	Social Studies> Cultural anthropology: Various living cultures of the world Story	Art>Music: Instruments in the orchestra Story	Social Studies> Life safety: Learning and using outdoor survival skills Story	Social Studies> History: The California Gold Rush Report	Social Studies & Science> Psychology: Psychology in everyday life Story	Literature> World classics: The Merchant of Venice Story
Book 9	Social Studies> Jobs: Interviews about jobs Report	Science>Scientific technology: Developments in technology in different times Story	Social Studies> Politics>Election: Running for 3rd grade class president Story	Literature> World classics: Stories of Sherlock Holmes Story	Literature> World classics: Adrift in the Pacific Story	Social Studies> History & People: Great world leaders in history Report
Book 10	Literature>Traditional fairy tale: Eastern and Western folk tales on the same theme Story	Sports>Winter sports: Various aspects of some Winter Olympic sports Report	Literature> World classics: Short stories by O. Henry Story	Sports> Ball games: Various aspects of popular ball games Report	Social Studies> History: Famous events that changed world history Report	Art & Social Studies> Art: Stories about the creation, distribution, and preservation of paintings Report

* 10 books in each level will be published.

How to Use This Book

• Before Reading

You can easily find the topic and what kind of story you are about to read.

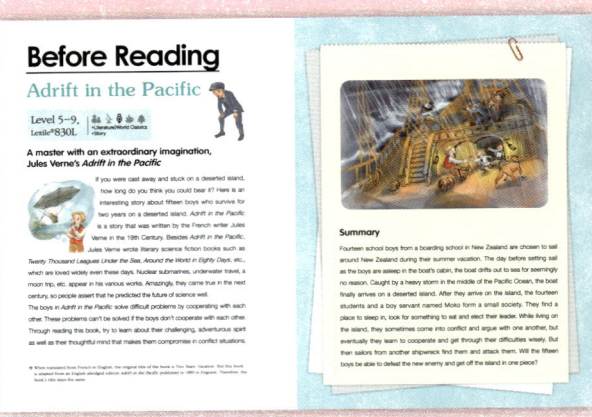

• The text

All the stories were written by professional writers from the U.S. and England, so you will read authentic and appropriate English sentences and expressions in every book in the series.

• Pop Quiz

Check out right away if you understand what you have just read by solving a pop quiz that checks your comprehension.

• Key Words

The key words and expressions on each page are listed for you to easily study them.

• Aha! Tips

Download free Korean explanations at *www.ihappyhouse.co.kr* for all of the sentences marked with "Aha!". These explain cultural, scientific, and economic knowledge or they deal with aspects of English such as grammatical structures or idiomatic expressions. There are lots of "Aha! Tips" to help you understand the text.

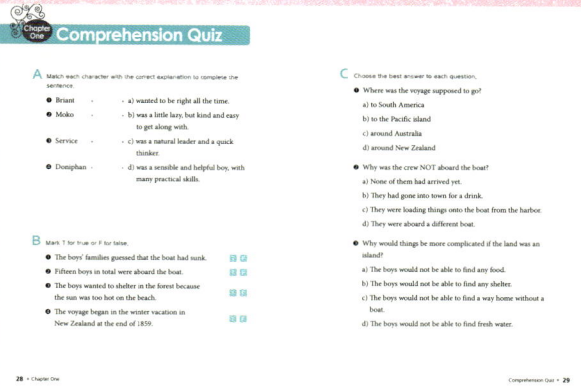

•Comprehension Quiz

After reading one chapter, solve various questions to find out if you fully understand the content.

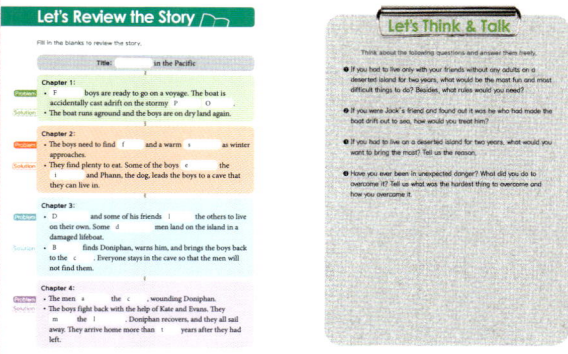

•Let's Review the Story /
•Let's Think & Talk

Fill in the blanks in the organizer to summarize the whole story. Express your own thinking and feelings about the story by answering the questions. You can build up logic and reasoning skills for your essay examinations in the future.

Appendix

Audio CD

In the CD audio book form, the texts are read vividly by American professional voice actors. (MP3 files downloaded for free)

After-reading Test

Solve an additionally provided After-reading Test for each book.

The Korean translation, Answer Keys, a Word Quiz, a Word List, and Aha! Tips for each book

You can download them for free at *www.ihappyhouse.co.kr* or *www.darakwon.co.kr*

Before Reading

Adrift in the Pacific

Level 5–9,
Lexile® 830L

•Literature⟩World Classics
•Story

A master with an extraordinary imagination, Jules Verne's *Adrift in the Pacific*

If you were cast away and stuck on a deserted island, how long do you think you could bear it? Here is an interesting story about fifteen boys who survive for two years on a deserted island. *Adrift in the Pacific* is a story that was written by the French writer Jules Verne in the 19th Century. Besides *Adrift in the Pacific*, Jules Verne wrote literary science fiction books such as *Twenty Thousand Leagues Under the Sea*, *Around the World in Eighty Days*, etc., which are loved widely even these days. Nuclear submarines, underwater travel, a moon trip, etc. appear in his various works. Amazingly, they came true in the next century, so people assert that he predicted the future of science well.

The boys in *Adrift in the Pacific* solve difficult problems by cooperating with each other. These problems can't be solved if the boys don't cooperate with each other. Through reading this book, try to learn about their challenging, adventurous spirit as well as their thoughtful mind that makes them compromise in conflict situations.

✣ When translated from French to English, the original title of the book is *Two Years' Vacation*. But this book is adapted from an English abridged edition *Adrift in the Pacific* published in 1889 in England. Therefore, the book's title stays the same.

Summary

Fourteen school boys from a boarding school in New Zealand are chosen to sail around New Zealand during their summer vacation. The day before setting sail as the boys are asleep in the boat's cabin, the boat drifts out to sea for seemingly no reason. Caught by a heavy storm in the middle of the Pacific Ocean, the boat finally arrives on a deserted island. After they arrive on the island, the fourteen students and a boy servant named Moko form a small society. They find a place to sleep in, look for something to eat and elect their leader. While living on the island, they sometimes come into conflict and argue with one another, but eventually they learn to cooperate and get through their difficulties wisely. But then sailors from another shipwreck find them and attack them. Will the fifteen boys be able to defeat the new enemy and get off the island in one piece?

Contents

Adrift in the Pacific

Adrift in the Pacific

Chapter One

A Storm and a Strange Land

It was the summer vacation in New Zealand at the end of 1859, and fourteen boys were all very excited.

They all attended a school in New Zealand for the sons of wealthy families, and had been chosen to go on a sea voyage. They were going to cruise around the whole of New Zealand to advance their education.

The voyage was expected to take six weeks. The boys couldn't think of a better way to spend their vacation!

On the boat, there was a crew of seven sailors. There was also a cook, and a boy called Moko. He was a servant on the boat.

When the boys went aboard the boat, most of the crew had gone into town for a drink. The captain wasn't there yet. Only Moko and one sailor were there to greet them.

Once the boys were in bed, the sailor left Moko in charge and he went into town, too. But Moko was too tired to stay awake.

KEY WORDS

- strange
- land
- New Zealand
- at the end of
- attend
- wealthy
- choose (choose-chose-chosen)
- go on a sea voyage (cf. voyage)
- be going to + Verb
- cruise
- whole
- advance
- education
- be expected to + Verb (cf. expect)
- take (take-took-taken)

- week
- better
- crew
- sailor
- servant
- go aboard (cf. aboard)
- go for a drink (go-went-gone)
- captain
- yet
- greet
- once
- leave (leave-left-left)
- in charge
- too ... to ~
- stay awake (cf. stay)

Somehow, the rope that tied the boat to the harbor wall became unfastened. Nobody noticed the boat slipping out onto the water.

Moko was the first to wake up, and he shouted as loud as he could to wake up the others. Gordon, Briant, Doniphan, and a few others woke up. They called for help, but they were too far away for anyone to hear them.

The wind pushed the boat right out to sea, toward the Pacific Ocean. The boys saw a light coming toward them and yelled for help. It was a steam ship, huge and noisy.

Nobody aboard noticed the tiny boat or heard the boys' cries above the noise of their own engine.

KEY WORDS

- somehow
- tie (↔ untie)
- harbor
- become (become-became-become)
- unfastened
- nobody
- notice
- slip out
- shout
- as loud as
- call for (cf. call)

- far away
- the Pacific Ocean
- light
- yell
- steam ship
- huge
- noisy
- tiny
- above (↔ below)
- engine

The steam ship came so close to the boys' boat that it knocked off a piece of the nameboard.

Luckily, the small boat stayed upright instead of sinking, but the steam ship sailed past… and the boys sailed on into a rising storm.

Of course, the boys' families searched for them, but when they found the piece of nameboard, they guessed that the boat had sunk. Broken-hearted, they gave up the search.

POP QUIZ

Mark T for true or F for false.

The steam ship came so close to the boys' boat that it found the boys.　　　　T / F

KEY WORDS

- so … that ~
- knock off
- piece
- nameboard
- luckily
- upright
- instead of
- sink (sink-sank-sunk)
- sail
- rising (cf. rise)
- search for (cf. search)
- guess
- broken-hearted

- give up (give-gave-given)
- several
- find oneself (find-found-found)
- yet another
- endurance
- through
- crashing
- rough
- nothing to do but + Verb
- hold on (to) (hold-held-held)
- tight
- tear (tear-tore-torn)

Several weeks later, the boys found themselves in yet another storm.

Each day was a test of endurance as the boat sailed on through the crashing waves.

When the weather was rough like this, there was nothing to do but hold on tight and hope that the sails would not tear.

On the deck stood Gordon, Briant, Doniphan, and Moko, all trying to steer the ship by holding onto the wheel. Doniphan looked white with fear, while Moko's skin was as dark as the clouds above them. These four were all aged between twelve and fourteen.

In the rooms below the deck were eleven younger boys and a dog.

KEY WORDS

- deck
- stand (stand-stood-stood)
- try to + *Verb*
- steer
- wheel
- fear
- while

- aged
- between
- suddenly
- peer
- gloom
- question
- lord

- certainly (*cf*. certain)
- seem
- reply
- mast
- strip
- horizon

Suddenly, Moko yelled, "Land! I can see land!"

"Are you sure?" asked Doniphan, peering through the early morning gloom.

He always questioned everything that other people said, wanting to be right. Some of the others called him 'Lord Doniphan' because he certainly seemed to think that he was better than everyone else.

"Yes, I'm certain," replied Moko. "Look, to the right of the mast."

"It is land!" cried Briant. "It really is!"

Then, they all saw a long, low strip of land on the horizon.

Briant was a natural leader and a quick thinker. He reasoned that if the boat was going to crash onto any rocks, everyone would be safer on deck.

He opened the door that led down to the rooms below the deck, and yelled, "Come up on deck, all of you." Immediately, the dog jumped out and all eleven boys followed.

The youngest ones began to scream when they saw the waves around them.

Suddenly, there was a great thud. The boat had run aground on the rocks. Waves swirled around it and lifted it clear again, but they only carried it further in and dumped it onto some sand in shallow water.

The boat had reached the land, but what kind of land was it? It could be a continent, in which case they could travel overland until they reached some kind of settlement such as a village or town.

But if it was an island, things would be more complicated because there was no way of leaving without a seaworthy boat.

KEY WORDS

- natural
- leader
- quick thinker (*cf.* quick)
- reason
- crash (onto)
- safer
- lead down to (lead-led-led)
- immediately
- follow
- youngest
- begin (begin-began-begun)
- scream

- thud
- run aground (run-ran-run)
- swirl
- lift
- clear
- carry
- further
- dump
- shallow
- reach
- continent
- travel

- overland
- until
- settlement
- such as
- village
- island
- things (*cf.* thing)
- complicated
- without
- seaworthy

The boys scrambled out of the boat and waded ashore,
pulling the boat with them so that it was out of the water.
It was battered and broken up, so there was no way of sailing
away from here. The shore was deserted.

KEY WORDS

- scramble
- wade
- ashore

- so that
- battered
- **break up** (break-broke-broken)

- shore
- deserted

"First, we need food and shelter," said Briant. "Then, we can work out what to do next."

Briant and Gordon walked up the beach and into the forest, where they found a cliff. They followed the cliff until they reached a stream.

On the other side of the stream was a marsh. It was clear that there was no place to shelter there.

Disappointed, the boys returned to the wrecked boat. They would have to shelter there for now.

Fortunately, the bedding, clothes, and cooking things were still on the boat. There was even food, which Moko made into a good meal.

KEY WORDS

- shelter
- work out
- cliff
- stream
- on the other side of

- marsh
- disappointed
- return
- wrecked
- have to + *Verb*

- for now
- fortunately
- bedding
- still
- meal

Moko was a very sensible and helpful boy, with many practical skills that he used to make everyone safe and comfortable.

Everyone seemed to be surprisingly cheerful, except Briant's younger brother, Jack, who was quite miserable.

Next morning, the boys looked at their food supplies.

Briant and Gordon judged that they had enough to last for two months, but they didn't know how long they might have to survive in this place, so they needed to find other sources of food.

POP QUIZ

Which boy felt miserable?
ⓐ Jack
ⓑ Doniphan

KEY WORDS

- sensible
- helpful
- practical
- skill
- used to + *Verb*
- comfortable

- surprisingly
- cheerful
- except
- quite
- miserable
- food supply (*cf.* supply)

- judge
- enough
- last
- might + *Verb*
- survive
- source

They gathered the eggs of seabirds and caught some fish using the fishing lines from the boat. They also found shellfish on the rocks near the sea.

As well as food, there were other supplies on board, such as ropes, sails, maps, and matches. There were plenty of warm, waterproof clothes.

There were also some guns, though Briant hoped that they would never have to use those!

They decided that they must try to find shelter in the forest. The weather on the beach was too wild, and they could not stay there when winter came.

Briant, Doniphan, Service, and Wilcox set out to explore, taking the dog, Phann, with them.

Gordon, who was very sensible, stayed behind to look after the other boys.

Service was a good-hearted boy, a little lazy but generally kind and easy to get along with.

The four explorers set off along the beach. They climbed up the cliff with some difficulty, and scrambled down the other side, where they found more forest. The boys walked and walked. The forest seemed to have no end.

POP QUIZ

How many boys set out to explore?
ⓐ four
ⓑ five

KEY WORDS

- **set out** (set-set-set)
- **explore**
- **stay behind**
- **look after**
- **good-hearted**
- **generally**
- **get along with** (get-got-gotten)(*cf.* along)
- **set off**
- **difficulty**

- in the middle of
- come across
- **make a discovery** (*cf.* discovery)
- a sort of
- wash
- suggest
- prove
- nearby

In the middle of the forest, they came across a river, where they made a surprising discovery.

"Look at this," said Service as he peered at some rocks. "Someone has made a sort of bridge with these rocks."

"The rocks could have been washed there by a storm," suggested Briant. "It doesn't prove that there are people nearby."

But the boys were very watchful that night as they settled down to camp in the forest. They decided not to make a fire, in case there were people around. They didn't want to attract anyone's attention, but it meant that they spent a very cold night outside, with only cold food to eat.

The next morning, the boys woke up early and went a little way into the forest to explore it. To everyone's surprise, they discovered that they had been sleeping close to a hut made out of leaves and wood.

KEY WORDS

- watchful
- settle down (*cf.* settle)
- camp
- make a fire
- in case
- attract
- attention
- mean (mean-meant-meant)
- to one's surprise
- discover

- close to
- hut
- made out of
- leaves
- surely
- whisper
- as though
- anxiously
- cannibal

"Surely that means that there are people nearby." whispered
Doniphan.

"The hut looks old, as though it has not been used for a long
time," said Briant.

"But there might be people around," said Service, anxiously,
"and we don't know if they are good or bad." 📖
Aha!

"I hope they aren't cannibals." whispered Wilcox.

A Match each character with the correct explanation to complete the sentence.

❶ Briant •   • a) wanted to be right all the time.

❷ Moko •   • b) was a little lazy, but kind and easy to get along with.

❸ Service •   • c) was a natural leader and a quick thinker.

❹ Doniphan •   • d) was a sensible and helpful boy, with many practical skills.

B Mark T for true or F for false.

❶ The boys' families guessed that the boat had sunk.   T F

❷ Fifteen boys in total were aboard the boat.   T F

❸ The boys wanted to shelter in the forest because the sun was too hot on the beach.   T F

❹ The voyage began in the winter vacation in New Zealand at the end of 1859.   T F

Choose the best answer to each question.

❶ Where was the voyage supposed to go?

a) to South America

b) to the Pacific island

c) around Australia

d) around New Zealand

❷ Why was the crew NOT aboard the boat?

a) None of them had arrived yet.

b) They had gone into town for a drink.

c) They were loading things onto the boat from the harbor.

d) They were aboard a different boat.

❸ Why would things be more complicated if the land was an island?

a) The boys would not be able to find any food.

b) The boys would not be able to find any shelter.

c) The boys would not be able to find a way home without a boat.

d) The boys would not be able to find fresh water.

Chapter Two

Discoveries and a Secret

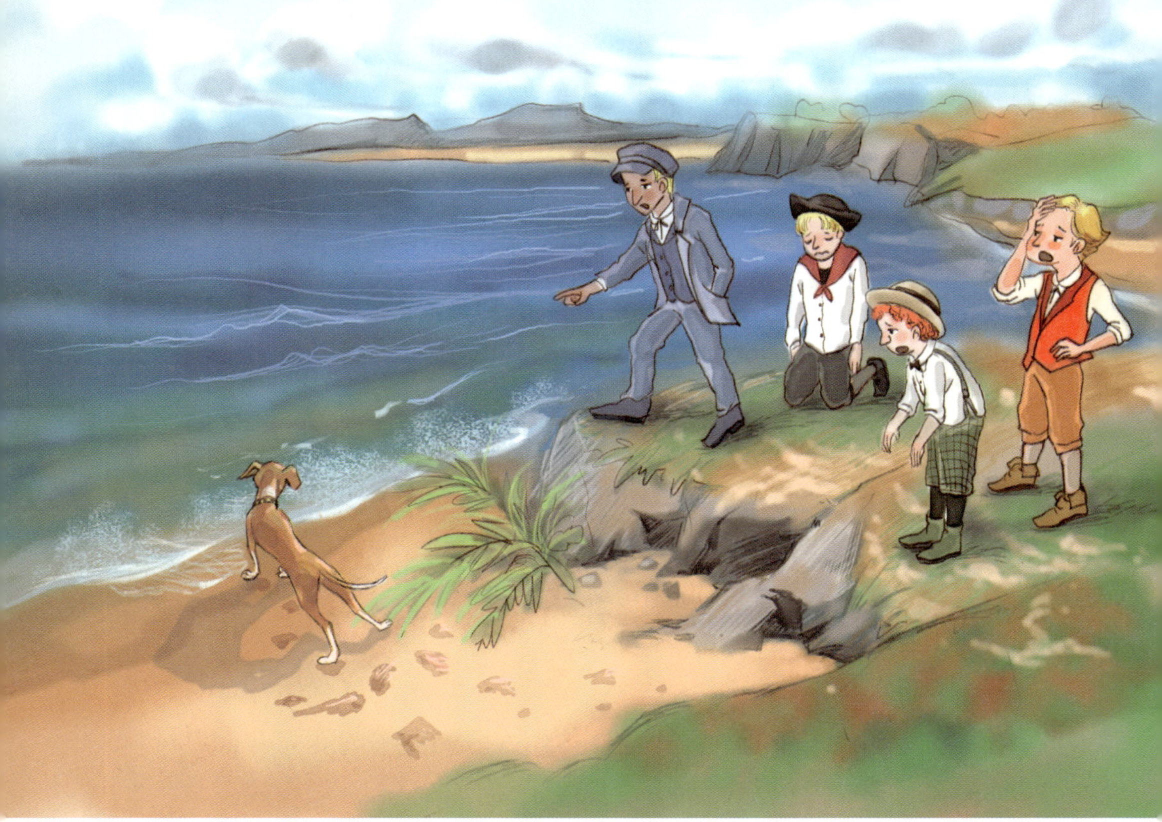

The boys finally came to the end of the forest, and beyond it they found a sandy beach and a huge expanse of water. "It is an island," exclaimed Briant, half sick with disappointment. Aha!

"Look, here is the sea and there is no sign of a shore on the other side."

"I don't agree," said Doniphan, who didn't agree with Briant on much at all. "I think we should explore a bit further."

▲ island

Even though Briant was getting increasingly angry with Doniphan and his argumentative ways, he agreed.

The boys set off again, looking warily around them for wild animals or people.

Mark T for true or F for false.

Briant was getting increasingly angry with Wilcox.   T / F

KEY WORDS

- secret
- finally
- beyond
- sandy
- expanse
- exclaim

- half
- sick
- disappointment
- sign
- agree
- not at all

- should + *Verb*
- a bit
- even though
- increasingly
- argumentative
- warily

At last, they spotted a sandy shore beyond the water. They climbed up a small hill and Doniphan reached the top first. "It's not the sea at all," he said. "It's a huge lake, which means that we're not on an island, Briant."

Briant was still not sure about that, but he kept quiet for now, since Gordon had asked him before they left to try not to argue with Doniphan.

When they came back to the lake shore near the forest, Phann began to behave strangely. He ran toward a group of trees on the lake shore, barking and running back and forth between the trees and the boys.

It seemed that he wanted the boys to follow him, so they did. They found a tree with some letters and a year scratched on it.

FB

1807

POP QUIZ

What was the year scratched onto the tree?
ⓐ 1807   ⓑ 1859

KEY WORDS

- spot
- climb up
- keep quiet (keep-kept-kept)
- since

- argue
- behave
- strangely
- a group of

- bark
- back and forth
- letter
- scratch

The boys looked at it thoughtfully, but as they were trying to figure out what it all meant, Phann hurried away again and disappeared.

They heard him barking again, and followed him to some bushes at the base of a cliff.

Behind the bushes, hidden by branches that had grown across it, was the entrance to a cave.

"Be careful," said Doniphan. "There could be something — or someone — living in there!"

"We must check that the air is good to breathe, too," warned Briant. Aha!

KEY WORDS

- thoughtfully
- figure out
- hurry away
- disappear (↔ appear)
- bush
- base

- hide (hide-hid-hidden)
- branch
- entrance
- cave
- breathe
- warn

- carefully
- cautiously
- floor
- tin
- jug
- stop + *Verb*-ing

The boys went into the cave, walking carefully and breathing cautiously. The floor was dry and sandy, and the air was good to breathe.

To their surprise, there was a table inside, with a tin cup and a jug on it. There was even a clock on the wall, though it had stopped telling the time long ago.

It was clear to the boys that someone had lived here at some time, and it was hard to tell how long ago.

Outside, Phann was still barking.

The boys went out to see him and, to their horror, there was a skeleton lying on the bank of the river!  The boys were shocked at the sight.

This person must have been shipwrecked and must have lived in the cave, but the fact that his skeleton was still here meant that he had never managed to leave this place.

POP QUIZ

Mark T for true or F for false.

The boys found the skeleton lying in the cave.

T / F

KEY WORDS

- to one's horror (*cf.* horror)
- skeleton
- lie (lie-lay-lain)
- bank
- be shocked at
- sight
- shipwreck

- fact
- manage to + *Verb*
- feel a chill (feel-felt-felt)
- thought
- either
- come up with (come-came-come)
- plan

Briant felt a chill at the thought, because it meant that the
boys might never leave the island either.

Still, if this man could live in the cave, then they could live in
the cave, too, until they came up with a better plan.

The cave was dry, and big enough for all the boys to live in.

When they went back inside for another search, they found a book with a lot of writing in it. The words were impossible to read, except a name: François Baudoin. FB: the same initials as those carved on the tree!

"The skeleton must be François Baudoin," said Briant.

Doniphan suddenly shouted, "I've found a map! It was hidden here between the pages of the book!"

"François must have drawn it," said Briant, leaning over Doniphan's shoulder to take a closer look.

It was a map of the whole area, proving that it really was an island.

"So you were right, Briant," said Doniphan, gloomily. "This place is an island and therefore we cannot leave here without a boat."

POP QUIZ

What did Doniphan find in the book?
ⓐ a map
ⓑ a letter

KEY WORDS

- **a lot of** (= lots of)
- **writing**
- **word**
- **impossible** (↔ possible)
- **name**
- **initial**

- **carve**
- **lean over**
- **take a look** (= have a look)
- **area**
- **gloomily**
- **therefore**

The boys dug a grave for François and said a prayer for his soul there. Then, they hurried back to tell Gordon about the cave.

On the way back, they got lost, even though they tried to use the map to find the way back.

Night fell, and they faced another night in the forest with no way of knowing where they were.

Then, in the silence of the night, there was a sudden bang and a flash of light. Gordon had sent up a flare from the boat to signal the way back! The boys hurried thankfully in the direction of the rocket and got back to the boat within an hour.

KEY WORDS

- **dig** (dig-dug-dug)
- **grave**
- **say a prayer** (*cf.* prayer)
- **soul**
- **on the way back**
- **get lost**
- **fall** (fall-fell-fallen)
- **face**
- **silence**

- **sudden**
- **bang**
- **flash**
- **flare**
- **signal**
- **thankfully**
- **in the direction of**
- **rocket**
- **get back**

- **within**
- **French**
- **build** (build-built-built)
- **raft**
- **unusual** (↔ usual)
- **be known for**
- **confident**

Everyone thought it was a good idea to go and live in the cave, which they called French Cave because a French man had lived there.

They built a raft to carry everything to the cave and they sailed it all the way along the river from the beach to the cave.

Everyone was very excited when they got there, except Briant's brother, Jack, who still seemed quiet and sad. It was very unusual for him, because he had always been known for being a happy and confident boy.

"You're hiding something," Briant whispered to Jack, "or are you ill?"

Jack just shook his head, but refused to say anything about it.

The boys brought in all the beds and tables from the boat, so they were nice and cozy in the cave.

Moko made a good meal and there was a party atmosphere in the cave that night.

As the days went on, the boys settled into life at French Cave. Doniphan stirred up arguments all the time, but Gordon managed to calm everything down.

He gave lessons from the books that he had brought from the boat, and everyone sat and listened.

The boys made the cave bigger with their tools from the boat.

Luckily, the rock was soft enough for them to chip away at it and they soon dug it away.

They also made two narrow windows in the walls so that they could look out through them and fresh air could flow into the cave.

The boys were all safe despite floods and storms outside.

KEY WORDS

- ill
- shake one's head (shake-shook-shaken)
- refuse
- bring (bring-brought-brought)
- cozy
- atmosphere
- go on
- settle into
- stir up
- argument

- all the time
- calm ~ down
- give lessons
- tool
- chip away
- narrow
- fresh
- flow
- despite (= in spite of)
- flood

Now that they had a bigger cave to live in, the boys decided to name the main parts of the island.

"Let us call it Chairman Island," suggested Gordon, "after the chairman of the board who runs our school. He arranged the voyage for us, so we shall name the island after him."

They named the beach where the boat was wrecked Schooner Bay, because a schooner was the type of boat they had sailed in.  (Aha!)

▲ bay

"We need a leader," said Briant, "and I think it should be you, Gordon." Most boys agreed with Briant, so Gordon became the leader on Chairman Island.

KEY WORDS

- now that
- main
- let (let-let-let)
- chairman
- run a school
- arrange
- shall + *Verb*

- name after
- schooner
- bay
- type
- turn
- bitterly
- deep

- busy + *Verb*-ing
- learn
- melt
- hunt
- be good at + *Verb*-ing
- particularly
- shoot (shoot-shot-shot)

Winter came and the weather turned bitterly cold. The snow was so deep that nobody could leave the cave.

Gordon kept everyone busy washing clothes and learning their lessons from the books.

When the snow melted, the boys went out and hunted for food. There were plenty of animals around the island, and Doniphan was particularly good at using the guns to shoot them.

Briant talked about building a boat so that they could leave the island, but Gordon liked living there and made more plans to keep everyone comfortable.

Gordon was a good leader, but Doniphan was jealous of him and Briant, so he began to complain about both of them. One day, he even got into a fight with Briant over a game. Gordon had to come and separate the two of them.

"Why should you be the leader, Gordon?" growled Doniphan. "I could be a better leader than you, and I think I should be the leader."

His friends, Wilcox and Webb, and his cousin, Cross, agreed with him. They went around trying to persuade the other boys that Doniphan should be the new leader.

Cross had always admired Doniphan and did everything that his cousin said. Webb and Wilcox were only twelve, and they were not particularly clever. They liked to quarrel with one another and to persuade other people to do their work for them.

These were the kind of boys that Doniphan gathered around him — boys who would do what he told them without questioning him.

Some of the other boys listened, and some ignored Doniphan and his friends.

KEY WORDS

- be jealous of
- complain
- get into a fight
- separate
- growl
- go around
- persuade
- admire
- clever
- quarrel
- one another
- the kind of
- ignore

Briant was still worried about his brother, Jack, who was
becoming sadder and sadder.

At last, Jack spoke to Briant about his secret.

"You might forgive me," he said, "but I don't think the other
boys will."

"But what have you done?" asked Briant.

"You will find out soon enough," said Jack, starting to cry.

The boys had gathered a few animals and birds by now.

They made some farm enclosures for them.

Moko cooked some wonderful food with eggs from the birds and milk from the vicuña, a creature like a llama.  He even managed to make a sugar syrup from the sap of a maple tree, so everyone ate well!

▲ vicuña

"I will go and explore the east side of the island," said Briant. "Then, I can see if any ships pass on that side."

He took Moko and Jack with him. They sailed in a small boat that they had brought from the larger, wrecked boat.

POP QUIZ

What animal provided milk to the boys?

ⓐ a llama
ⓑ a vicuña

KEY WORDS

- sadder
- forgive
  (forgive-forgave-forgiven)
- find out
- soon enough

- enclosure
- milk
- vicuña
- creature
- llama

- sap
- maple tree
- east
- pass

After a long journey along the river, they reached the eastern coast. There was a sandy beach with only a few rocks there, but no ships passed that way, even though they stayed watching all day.

Briant called the place Deception Bay because he felt as though the place had deceived him. He looked through his telescope and frowned as he saw something strange on the horizon. It looked like a cloud, but the sky was clear. Briant did not know what it was, even though Moko said that he could see it, too.

After a while, Briant and Jack went for a walk on their own, leaving Moko behind to wait for the tide to change so that they could sail their boat back to the cave.

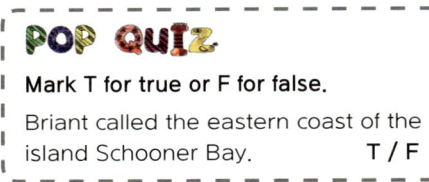

POP QUIZ

Mark T for true or F for false.

Briant called the eastern coast of the island Schooner Bay.   T / F

KEY WORDS

- journey
- eastern
- coast
- deception
- deceive

- look through
- telescope
- frown
- go for a walk
- on one's own

- leave ~ behind
- wait for
- tide

Moko couldn't help but overhear Briant and Jack talking about Jack's secret.

"You did it!" gasped Briant, his voice shocked.

"I'm sorry," said Jack, as he began to cry again.

"You must not tell the others," said Briant.

KEY WORDS

▪ can't help but + *Verb*   ▪ gasp
▪ **overhear** (overhear-overheard-overheard)

A Match the place related to the island and the word used for each place correctly.

❶ the bay on the east •
side of the island

 • a) French

❷ the island •

 • b) Schooner

❸ the bay where •
the boat landed

 • c) Chairman

❹ the cave •

 • d) Deception

B Fill in each blank with the right word below.

shipwrecked	impossible	shocked	hidden

❶ The boys were _____ at the sight of the skeleton.

❷ The man, François Baudoin, must have been _____.

❸ The words in the book were _____ to read.

❹ The map was _____ in the pages of the book.

C Choose the best answer to each question.

❶ Why did NOT Jack want to tell anyone his secret?

   a) He didn't think the other boys would forgive him.

   b) He didn't think that Briant would forgive him.

   c) He didn't think that anyone would want to hear it.

   d) He didn't think that anyone would believe it.

❷ How did the boys carry everything from the boat to the cave?

   a) They carried it on their backs.

   b) They loaded it onto the backs of animals.

   c) They made a cart and pulled it along.

   d) They made a raft and sailed it along the river.

❸ What was NOT right about the cave?

   a) The floor was dry.

   b) There was a clock on the wall.

   c) There was a skeleton in the corner.

   d) There was a tin cup on the table.

Chapter Three

Unwanted Visitors

When Briant, Jack, and Moko got back to the cave, life went on as usual.

Doniphan kept arguing with everyone and he complained about everything.

By now, Gordon had been the leader of the island for a whole year.

"It's time to elect a new leader," said Doniphan, who hoped that he would be elected as the new leader.

But Briant was elected instead, and all through another winter, Doniphan grew angrier and angrier.

KEY WORDS

- unwanted
- visitor
- as usual
- keep + *Verb*-ing
- it's time to + *Verb*
- elect

- angrier (*cf. comparative form + and + comparative form*)
- no longer
- be tired of
- snap at
- perfectly

When summer came again, Doniphan could stand it no longer.

"I'm tired of doing what you say," he snapped at Briant, and he took Cross, Wilcox, and Webb away to Deception Bay.

"We don't need the others," he said. "We can live perfectly well here on our own."

▲ thunder and lightning

The first night at Deception Bay was very stormy, with crashing thunder and flashing lightning.

As Doniphan and his friends sheltered in the forest at the edge of the beach, Wilcox noticed something strange.

"What's that?" he shouted, pointing at a large, dark shape on the beach.

It looked like a boat. The boys rushed out to have a look, and found that it was a boat.

POP QUIZ

Who first noticed the boat on the beach at Deception Bay?

ⓐ Doniphan
ⓑ Wilcox

KEY WORDS

- stormy
- thunder
- flash
- lightning
- at the edge of
- point
- shape
- rush

Two bodies lay next to it on the sand. The boys thought that they should stay and try to help, but the storm was so fierce that they were too afraid. They hurried back to the shelter of the trees.

During the night, they thought they heard distant cries, but when the lightning stopped, it was too dark to see anything.

In the morning, when it was light, the boys went to the boat to have a look. But the two bodies had disappeared, and there was no sign that they had been dragged away by wild animals.

"The tide must have washed them away," said Doniphan. The boat was smashed on one side, but at the back they could still read a name: "Severn".

The words "San Francisco" were also written on it, indicating the port from which it had sailed.

"It's come from America," said Doniphan. "I wonder if that means that we are close to the coast of America."

▲ San Francisco

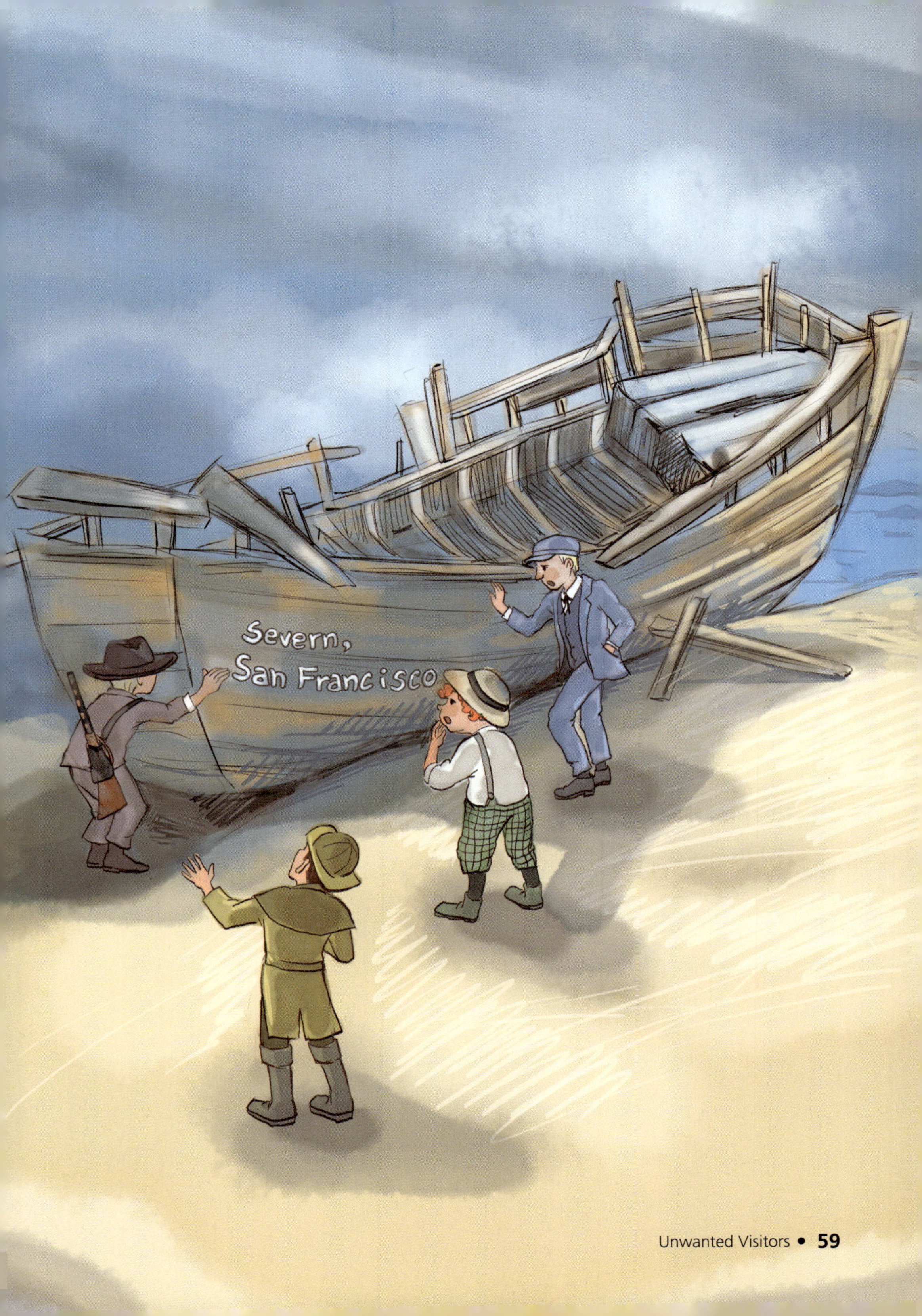
Severn,
San Francisco

Back at French Cave, everyone was sad. They wished that
Doniphan and his friends had not gone away.

But there were other things to think about, such as the need
for a signal in case any boats passed by the island.

"Let's make a kite," suggested Briant. "It will go high into
the sky and if any ships pass, they will see it."

The younger boys were very excited about Briant's idea and
they had a wonderful time making a huge kite.

▲ winch

They attached it to the heavy metal winch from the boat. They anchored it to the ground so that it could not float away.

Just as the boys got ready to launch the kite, Phann went toward the forest, barking yet again.

"What has he found this time?" asked Gordon, as all the boys followed the dog.

This time, Phann led them to a woman, who was lying under a tree, unconscious but alive. They took her back to the cave and wet her lips with some brandy.

POP QUIZ

What did Briant want to make?
ⓐ a kite
ⓑ a balloon

KEY WORDS

- go away
- pass by
- kite
- attach
- metal

- winch
- anchor
- float away
- get ready to + *Verb*
- launch

- unconscious
- alive
- wet
- brandy

When the woman, who appeared to be in her forties, woke
up, she told them her story.

"My name is Kate," she said. "I was a servant in America
when my employer and his wife took me on a voyage to
Chile in a boat called the 'Severn'."

Kate told the boys all about the crew of the "Severn." They
had killed the captain, Kate's employer, and his wife so that
they could take charge of the boat and everything on it.

Their leader was called Walston and most of the others were mostly bad men. They did what Walston told them to do, although one of them, called Forbes, was less cruel than the others. He persuaded them to spare Kate's life.

The men also spared the life of the ship's master, Evans, who was second in command to the captain. They needed him to navigate.

KEY WORDS

- in one's forties
- employer (↔ employee)
- Chile
- take charge of

- mostly
- less
- cruel
- spare

- master
- second in command
- navigate

Kate told the boys how the boat had caught fire and one man had died when he jumped overboard to escape from the flames.

Nobody knew how the fire had started, but it was so fierce that the entire ship burned up and sank. 📖 Aha!

Luckily, there was a lifeboat which they had jumped into. This was the boat that had washed ashore on Chairman Island, with the crew and Kate aboard.

Kate was thrown onto the beach when the lifeboat landed, and after a while she managed to get up and escape without being seen. The men probably thought that she was dead by now.

KEY WORDS

- catch fire
- overboard
- escape
- flame
- entire
- burn up
- lifeboat

- be thrown onto
  (*cf.* throw (throw-threw-thrown))
- probably
- dead
- horrified
- dangerous
- look for

Briant was horrified to hear that there were dangerous men
on the island!

"We must find Doniphan and the others," he cried. "We will
bring them back to the cave where they will be safer."

He and Moko set out to look for them, taking the boat along
the river and into the deep, dark forest.

Doniphan and his friends were camping in the forest, next to a flickering fire. A jaguar attacked Doniphan just at the moment that Briant and Moko arrived.

▲ jaguar

Wilcox grabbed his gun to shoot the jaguar, but Briant shouted, "Don't shoot!"

He slashed at the jaguar with his knife, injuring his shoulder as he did so.

The jaguar limped away, giving the boys a chance to escape.

"Come on!" gasped Briant, clutching his shoulder. "Let's go!"

"Thank you for saving my life," said Doniphan.

KEY WORDS

- flickering (*cf.* flicker)
- jaguar
- attack
- moment
- arrive

- grab
- slash
- injure
- limp
- chance

- Come on!
- clutch
- save one's life
- thank you for ~

Briant led them back to the boat, telling them about the dangerous men on the way.

"That is why I told you not to shoot, Wilcox," he explained. "The men might hear the shot and then they would know that they are not alone on the island."

Friends once more, Briant and Doniphan sailed the boat back to the cave and all fifteen boys were reunited.

Everyone had to be very careful not to be discovered. Briant did not allow them to go far from the cave in case the dangerous men found them.

POP QUIZ
Mark T for true or F for false.

Friends once more, Briant and Doniphan sailed the boat back to the wrecked boat.　　　　T / F

KEY WORDS

- explain
- alone
- once more
- reunite
- allow A to B

- crazy
- be able to + *Verb* (= can)
- exactly
- calculate
- how to + *Verb*

- support
- weight
- hang (hang-hung-hung)
- beneath

Then, Briant had a crazy idea.

"We can send this kite high into the air," he said. "A boy can go up with it. He will be able to see the whole island and will be able to see exactly where the men are."

The other boys agreed that this might be possible. They spent several days calculating how to support the weight of a boy, yet still allow the kite to fly. They made a basket to hang beneath the kite, so a boy could stand in it.

"Who will go up in it?" asked Gordon.

Jack volunteered, but so did Doniphan and some of the other boys.

"I must do it," insisted Jack, "because I want to make up for the wrong thing I did."

At last, he confessed that it was he who had untied the rope in the harbor in Auckland.  It was his fault that the boat had sailed away.

"It was meant to be a joke," he said in a small, sorry voice.

"Don't worry," said Doniphan. "It was a mistake and we will forgive you."

▲ Auckland

Now everyone realized why Jack had been so sad all this time. They all agreed that he could go up in the basket to view the island. But Briant didn't want his younger brother to do something so dangerous. So, when Jack was about to step into the basket, Briant jumped in first and gave the order to launch!

KEY WORDS

- volunteer
- insist
- make up for
- wrong
- confess
- Auckland

- fault
- be meant to + *Verb*
- joke
- mistake
- realize
- all this time

- view
- be about to + *Verb*
- step
- order

A Match each character with the correct explanation to complete the sentence.

❶ Kate •

❷ Forbes •

❸ Walston •

• a) was the leader of the crew who took over the "Severn."

• b) was thrown onto the beach when the lifeboat of the "Severn" landed.

• c) was less cruel than the other bad men on the crew of the "Severn."

B Fill in each blank with the right word below.

basket	sad	kite	weight

❶ The other boys agreed that it might be possible to send a _____ high into the air.

❷ The boys spent several days calculating how a kite could support the _____ of a boy.

❸ The boys made a _____ to hang beneath the kite, so a boy could stand in it.

❹ Now everyone realized why Jack had been so _____ all this time.

C Choose the best answer to each question.

❶ Why was everyone who left at the cave sad?

 a) They wanted to go home to New Zealand.

 b) Their cave had flooded during the storm.

 c) They had lost their dog, Phann.

 d) They wished that Doniphan and his friends had not gone away.

❷ Why did Briant want to make a kite?

 a) just for fun

 b) to act as a signal to passing ships

 c) to teach the younger boys about engineering

 d) to see which way the wind was blowing

❸ Why did Briant tell Wilcox NOT to shoot the jaguar?

 a) He thought that the jaguar might attack Wilcox.

 b) He wanted the jaguar to kill Doniphan.

 c) He didn't want the jaguar to get hurt.

 d) He didn't want the bad men to hear the sound of a gunshot.

Gun Battles and Goodbyes

Briant and the kite went up and up into the night sky, soon disappearing into the shadows.

A rope was tied to the kite so that it couldn't float away on its own.

Briant went up for ten minutes, until the rope pulled tight and he hovered above the island in the breeze. He had a great view of everything below.

The first thing he saw was the glow of a fire in the east, but it was too far away to be on the island.

POP QUIZ

When did Briant go up in the kite?
ⓐ during the night
ⓑ during the day

KEY WORDS

- gun battle (*cf.* battle)
- shadow
- hover

- breeze
- glow
- volcano

- perhaps
- remember
- glacier

"Is it a volcano?" he wondered. "Perhaps there is land over there!"

He remembered the white spot he had seen from Deception Bay and thought that perhaps there was an island with a glacier on it.

Then, he spotted another fire, much closer this time. It showed Briant that the men were still on Chairman Island. He pulled on the rope to tell the others that they could bring him and the kite back down to earth.

But, as the kite was lowered, there was a sudden gust of wind. It was strong enough to break the rope and knock Briant out of the basket!

Everyone screamed his name as he fell through the air, but luckily he landed in the lake and swam to the shore, unhurt. The kite, without his weight to hold it down, floated away into the sky like a gigantic bird.

POP QUIZ

Where did Briant land when he fell out of the kite?
ⓐ in the lake
ⓑ in the forest

KEY WORDS

- show
- earth (*cf.* (the) Earth)
- lower
- gust

- knock out of
- unhurt
- gigantic
- sound like

- thrilled
- after all
- mend

One stormy night, the boys and Kate were in the cave when they heard a voice outside, calling for help.

"It sounds like Evans," said Kate. "He is a good man, so it's safe to let him see us."

So the boys allowed Evans to come into the cave. He was thrilled to discover that Kate was alive after all.

"The lifeboat from the 'Severn' could be mended," he said, "but the men have no tools to do it, which is why they are still here."

"But we have tools," said Doniphan. "We could mend it!"

Evans told them that the dangerous men had found the kite, which had landed on the island. Then, they knew that someone else was on the island and soon after, they had discovered the cave.

They were planning an attack to take over the cave and steal everything in it.

Evans also told them that there was land nearby, so Briant had been right!

"This island is near the coast of South America," he said, "and its real name is Hanover Island."

So the boys began to make a plan to mend the lifeboat with their tools, if only they could get to it without the men stopping them. Then, they could sail away and perhaps find a way back home.

But first, they had to deal with the men, which was not going to be an easy task.

KEY WORDS

- soon after
- take over
- steal (steal-stole-stolen)

- South America
  (cf. south)
- if only

- get to
- deal with
- task

One evening, the bad men's attack began in a strangely quiet way, when two men came to the cave. They pretended to be shipwrecked sailors and said that their names were Forbes and Rock.

"Will you help us," Forbes cried, "by giving us food and shelter?"

The boys brought the men into the cave, pretending to believe their story. They wanted to capture the men.

Once the men were in the cave, the boys pushed them into a storeroom and kept them prisoner there. The men tried to escape, but Evans grabbed Forbes. Unfortunately, Rock escaped and

ran away, back to the other men.

POP QUIZ

Who did Forbes and Rock pretend to be?
ⓐ cannibals
ⓑ shipwrecked sailors

KEY WORDS

- pretend
- believe
- capture

- storeroom (*cf.* store)
- keep ~ prisoner
- unfortunately

- run away

The next day, there was the sound of gunshots, announcing the arrival of the other men.

The older boys rushed out of the cave and a great battle broke out.

There was a lot of fighting with guns and swords, and poor Doniphan was stabbed with a knife. He looked as though he might die.

"Get him back to the cave," shouted Gordon, but some of the men had already entered the cave.

Walston, the leader of the dangerous men, grabbed Jack. He tried to take Jack away on the boys' boat, which was moored on the river near the cave.

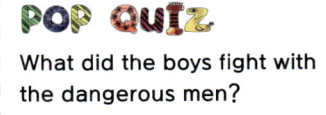

POP QUIZ

What did the boys fight with the dangerous men?

ⓐ sticks and stones
ⓑ guns and swords

KEY WORDS

- gunshot
- announce
- arrival
- break out
- fighting

- sword
- poor
- stab
- enter
- moor

Forbes rushed out of the cave and attacked Walston, but was killed in the struggle.

Everything seemed to be going wrong for the boys when something unexpected happened.

Moko had been hiding in a storeroom inside the cave, and remained undiscovered by the men.

Now, he came out of the storeroom with a gun. He fired some shots out through the windows of the cave.

Some of the men were killed and others were wounded.
They escaped into the forest, but died there of their wounds.
The boys knew this because Phann led them to the bodies.
The boys had won the battle, but Doniphan was seriously ill.
Kate dressed his wound with leaves and looked after him
through days and nights of pain and fever.

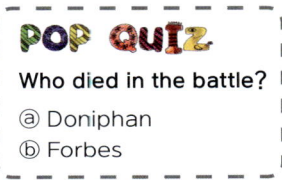

POP QUIZ

Who died in the battle?
ⓐ Doniphan
ⓑ Forbes

KEY WORDS

- struggle
- go wrong
- unexpected
- happen
- remain
- undiscovered
- wounded

- die of
- wound
- seriously
- dress
- day and night
- pain
- fever

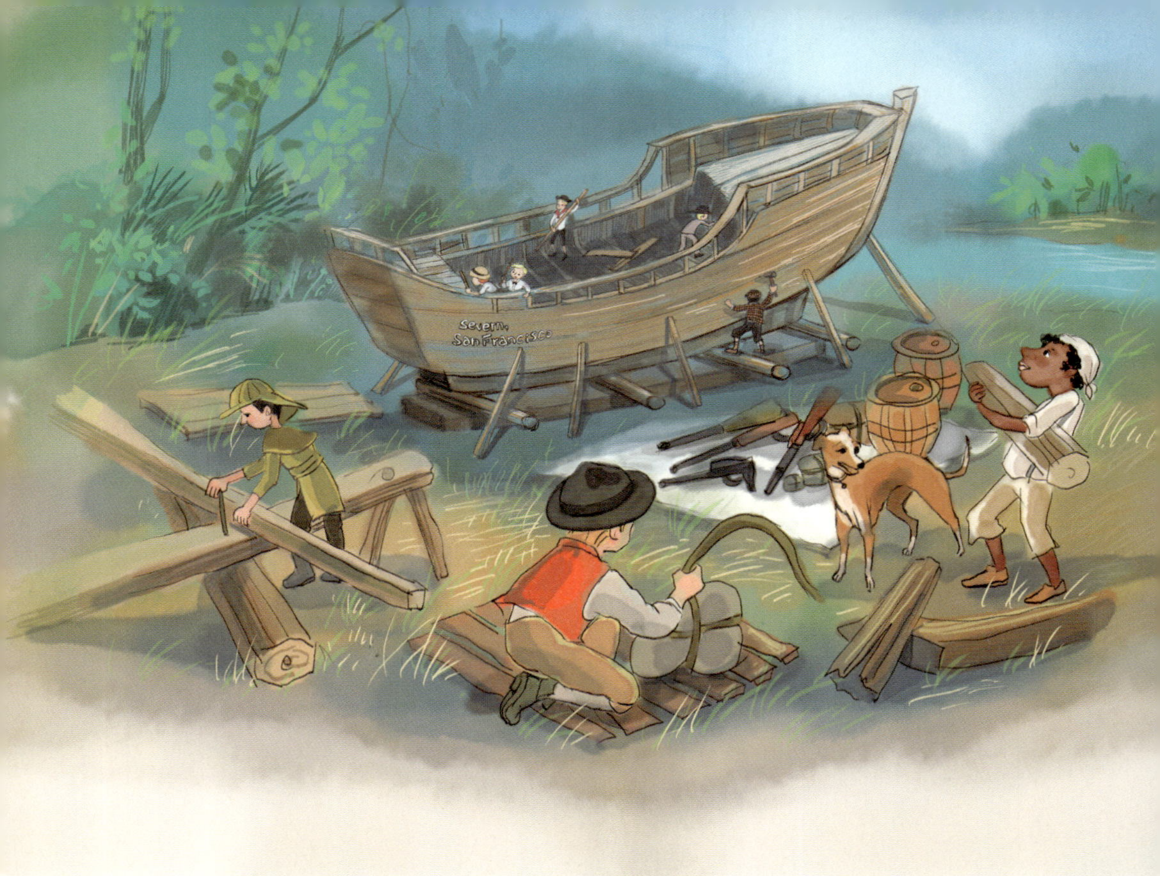

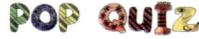

Meanwhile, the boys took tools, weapons, and provisions to Deception Bay.

They were ready to repair the lifeboat from the "Severn."

They worked hard on the repairs and, at last, the boat was ready.

POP QUIZ

Mark T for true or F for false.

The boys took tools, weapons, and provisions to French Cave to repair the lifeboat. T / F

Thanks to Kate's careful nursing, Doniphan was getting better and, after a while, he was well enough to come to Deception Bay to join the others.

After almost two years on the island, it was time to try and go home!

Before they left, the boys dug a grave for Forbes next to François Boudoin's grave. They said some prayers by the graves and thought for a while about these brave men.

POP QUIZ

Who was buried next to François Boudoin?

ⓐ Forbes
ⓑ Walston

KEY WORDS

- meanwhile
- weapon
- provisions
- be ready to + *Verb*

- repair
- hard
- thanks to
- nursing (*cf*, nurse)

- get better
- for a while

On the 5th February, the boys boarded the lifeboat, taking Kate and Evans with them. Even Phann stood proudly at the front of the boat as they departed.

After several days at sea, a steam ship picked them up and took them toward New Zealand, where their voyage had first begun.

On the 25th February, 1862, they finally arrived back in Auckland.

Their families had lost hope of seeing them alive and were overjoyed to see them.

"It's more than two years since we left," laughed Briant. "What a vacation we've had!"

POP QUIZ

How long the boys stay in the island?

ⓐ around 2 years
ⓑ around 1 year

KEY WORDS

- February
- proudly
- at the front of

- depart
- at sea
- pick up

- lose (lose-lost-lost)
- overjoyed
- more than

Chapter Four Comprehension Quiz

 A Match each character with the correct explanation to complete the sentence.

❶ Walston ·

· a) fired some shots out through the windows of the cave.

❷ Forbes ·

· b) ordered the boys to take Doniphan to the cave.

❸ Moko ·

· c) tried to take Jack away on the boat.

❹ Gordon ·

· d) rushed out of the cave but was killed in a struggle.

 B Mark T for true or F for false.

❶ The boys wanted to capture Forbes and Rock in a storeroom in the cave. T F

❷ Evans managed to escape from the cave. T F

❸ Doniphan was stabbed with a knife in the battle. T F

❹ Moko hid in a storeroom inside the cave during the battle. T F

C Choose the best answer to each question.

❶ How did the dangerous men know that the boys were on the island?

a) They had seen the boys' footprints.

b) They had heard the boys' voices.

c) They had found the boys' kite.

d) They had found the boys' boat.

❷ How did Briant describe their experience on the island?

a) a vacation   b) an adventure

c) a challenge   d) a nightmare

D Put the sentences in order.

❶ The boys arrived back in Auckland.

❷ The boys said some prayers by the graves.

❸ A steam ship took them toward New Zealand.

❹ Everyone got into the lifeboat and set out to sea.

_____ → _____ → _____ → _____

Let's Review the Story

Fill in the blanks to review the story.

Title: [_____] in the Pacific

Chapter 1:

Problem
- F[_____] boys are ready to go on a voyage. The boat is accidentally cast adrift on the stormy P[_____] O[_____].

Solution
- The boat runs aground and the boys are on dry land again.

Chapter 2:

Problem
- The boys need to find f[_____] and a warm s[_____] as winter approaches.

Solution
- They find plenty to eat. Some of the boys e[_____] the i[_____] and Phann, the dog, leads the boys to a cave that they can live in.

Chapter 3:

Problem
- D[_____] and some of his friends l[_____] the others to live on their own. Some d[_____] men land on the island in a damaged lifeboat.

Solution
- B[_____] finds Doniphan, warns him, and brings the boys back to the c[_____]. Everyone stays in the cave so that the men will not find them.

Chapter 4:

Problem
- The men a[_____] the c[_____], wounding Doniphan.

Solution
- The boys fight back with the help of Kate and Evans. They m[_____] the l[_____]. Doniphan recovers, and they all sail away. They arrive home more than t[_____] years after they had left.

Let's Think & Talk

Think about the following questions and answer them freely.

❶ If you had to live only with your friends without any adults on a deserted island for two years, what would be the most fun and most difficult things to do? Besides, what rules would you need?

❷ If you were Jack's friend and found out it was he who had made the boat drift out to sea, how would you treat him?

❸ If you had to live on a deserted island for two years, what would you want to bring the most? Tell us the reason.

❹ Have you ever been in unexpected danger? What did you do to overcome it? Tell us what was the hardest thing to overcome and how you overcame it.

Let's Review the Story

Title: Adrift in the Pacific

Chapter 1:

Problem
- Fifteen boys are ready to go on a voyage. The boat is accidentally cast adrift on the stormy Pacific Ocean .

Solution
- The boat runs aground and the boys are on dry land again.

Chapter 2:

Problem
- The boys need to find food and a warm shelter as winter approaches.

Solution
- They find plenty to eat. Some of the boys explore the island and Phann, the dog, leads the boys to a cave that they can live in.

Chapter 3:

Problem
- Doniphan and some of his friends leave the others to live on their own. Some dangerous men land on the island in a damaged lifeboat.

Solution
- Briant finds Doniphan, warns him, and brings the boys back to the cave . Everyone stays in the cave so that the men will not find them.

Chapter 4:

Problem
- The men attack the cave , wounding Doniphan.

Solution
- The boys fight back with the help of Kate and Evans. They mend the lifeboat . Doniphan recovers, and they all sail away. They arrive home more than two years after they had left.

Smart Readers: **Wise** & **Wide**

After-reading **Test**

- Adrift in the Pacific
- Level 5
- 29 Questions

(Vocabulary 7 / Reading Comprehension 16 /

Sentence Structure & Grammar 6)

1. What does "provisions" mean?
   ① weapons
   ② fishing equipment
   ③ food and drink
   ④ medicines

2. What does "cannibal" mean?
   ① a person who lives on islands
   ② a person who is very fierce
   ③ a person who eats other people
   ④ a person who is a ghost

3. What does "reunited" mean in the following sentence?

   > Briant and Doniphan sailed the boat back to the cave and all fifteen boys were <u>reunited</u>.

   ① friendly   ② enemies
   ③ together again   ④ happy

4. Which of the following is the wrong past tense form of the verb?
   ① shake – shook   ② fall – fell
   ③ hide – hid   ④ begin – begun

※ Choose the right word for each blank. (5~6)

5.
> "Thank you for _____ my life," said Doniphan.

① saving   ② having

③ floating   ④ flying

6.
> When the boys went _____ the boat, most of the crew had gone into town for a drink.

① disappeared   ② aboard

③ elected   ④ comfortable

7. What is the common word for the two blanks?

> • It was battered and broken _____, so there was no way of sailing away from here.
> • I must do it because I want to make _____ for the wrong thing I did.

① on   ② up

③ about   ④ of

8. In which season did the voyage begin?
    ① spring   ② summer
    ③ fall   ④ winter

9. Why did the boys' families give up searching for them?
　　① They assumed that the boat had sunk.
　　② They didn't care about the boys.
　　③ The weather was too stormy for them to search.
　　④ They knew that the boys would find their own way home.

10. Why did Briant call the younger boys up onto the deck?
　　① He wanted to see if they could see land.
　　② He wanted them to help to hold the wheel.
　　③ He wanted them to be safer if the boat crashed.
　　④ He wanted them to help with the sails.

11. Why did the boys need to look for food?
　　① There was no food on the boat.
　　② The food on the boat had gone bad.
　　③ Some of the boys did not like the food on the boat.
　　④ There was only enough food to last for two months.

12. Which of these things did Phann NOT discover?
　　① a tree with a year and letters scratched on it
　　② an old boat on the shore of the lake
　　③ a cave entrance hidden behind some branches
　　④ a skeleton lying on the bank of the river

13. Where did François Baudoin come from?
　① New Zealand
　② South America
　③ France
　④ United Kingdom

14. How did Gordon help the boys who explore the island to find their way back to the boat?
　① He fired a gun.
　② He shouted to them.
　③ He lit a fire.
　④ He sent up a flare.

15. Who was NOT excited to arrive at the cave?
　① Briant
　② Jack
　③ Doniphan
　④ Gordon

16. Why was Briant angry with Doniphan?
　① He didn't like it when other people were right and he was wrong.
　② He thought that Doniphan had put their lives in danger.
　③ He was tired of Doniphan arguing all the time.
　④ He blamed Doniphan for leading them the wrong way.

17. Why did Doniphan take Cross, Wilcox, and Webb to Deception Bay?
   ① He was tired of being told what to do by Jack.
   ② He thought he could live there without the others.
   ③ He wanted to try and get away from the island.
   ④ He wanted to live somewhere with more sunlight than the cave.

18. How did the boys stop the kite from floating away?
   ① They tied it to the winch.
   ② They tied it to a tree.
   ③ They tied it to a rock.
   ④ They tied it to the raft.

19. Why did Jack volunteer to go up in the basket with the kite?
   ① He wanted to make up for the wrong thing that he had done.
   ② He wanted to take a closer look at some birds.
   ③ He wanted to show that he was the bravest boy of them all.
   ④ He wanted to get away from all the other boys.

20. Why had the men from the "Severn" NOT left the island?
   ① They didn't know how to mend the lifeboat.
   ② The lifeboat had been washed away.
   ③ They liked the island so much that they wanted to stay.
   ④ They didn't have tools to mend the lifeboat.

21. Why did the boys allow Forbes and Rock into the cave?
　① The boys wanted to capture the men.
　② The boys didn't know that they were bad men.
　③ The boys hoped that the men would help them to mend the boat.
　④ The boys could not stop the men from entering the cave.

22. Where did the boys take their tools, weapons, and provisions?
　① Schooner Bay
　② Deception Bay
　③ French Cave
　④ into the forest

23. How many people boarded the lifeboat to try to leave the island?
　① fourteen
　② fifteen
　③ sixteen
　④ seventeen

※ Choose the wrong part of each sentence. (24~26)

24.
It was clear that there was no place sheltering there.
　①　　　② ③　　　　　　　　　④

25.

"We must checking that the air is good to breathe, too," warned Briant.
　　① 　　　　② 　　　　　　　　③ 　　　④

26.

But it was so fierce it the entire ship burned up and sank.
　　　　① ② ③ 　　　　　　　　　　　　　　④

※ Choose the correct sentence. (27～29)

27. ① And we don't know if they are good or bad.
　　② And we don't know if they will be good or bad.
　　③ And we don't know if they good or bad.
　　④ And we don't know if they could be good or bad.

28. ① There was even a clock on the wall, though it stopped tell the time long ago.
　　② There was even a clock on the wall, though it stopped to tell the time long ago.
　　③ There was even a clock on the wall, though it stopped old the time long ago.
　　④ There was even a clock on the wall, though it had stopped telling the time long ago.

29. ① The cave was dry, and big enough for all the boys to live in.

② The cave was dry, and enough big for all the boys to live in.

③ The cave was dry, and big for enough all the boys to live in.

④ The cave was dry, and enough to big for all the boys to live in.

Sarah J. Dodd

Sarah J. Dodd is an experienced primary school teacher who resides in the UK, but has also lived and taught in Australia. She has a PhD in Science and a certificate in Creative Writing. She has published several books for children: "An Angel Anyway" (Anyway Press, 2008) the "Little Angels" series (Lion Children's Books, 2009/10), "The Lion Picture Bible" (Lion Children's Books, 2015) and "Legs: the tale of a meerkat lost and found" (Lion Children's Books, 2015). Her poetry for children has also been highly commended and published in the anthology "Let in the Stars" (Manchester Metropolitan University, 2014).

She is currently working on further picture books for the very young, and a novel for older children.

 **5-9**

Adrift in the Pacific

Written by Jules Verne
Retold by Sarah J. Dodd
Illustrated by Hyeyeong Kim

First Published in March 2017

Editorial Manager: Juyon Choi
Editors: Jiyeong Park, Kyunghee Jang
Designer: Eunhee Lee
Cover Designer: Eunhee Lee

Published and distributed by

Darakwon Bldg., 64-1 Jandari-ro, Mapo-gu, Seoul, Korea 04031
Tel: 82-2-736-2031(ext. 250)   Fax: 82-2-732-2037
Homepage: www.ihappyhouse.co.kr
Publisher: Kyudo Chung

ISBN: 978-89-6653-510-1 18740 / 978-89-6653-156-1 18740(set)

[Components]
• 1 Audio CD (Recording Studio: Aram)
• Answer Keys & Korean Translation: Free download at www.ihappyhouse.co.kr